SPACE OUT!

Make Me Laugh!

SPACE OUT!
jokes about outer space

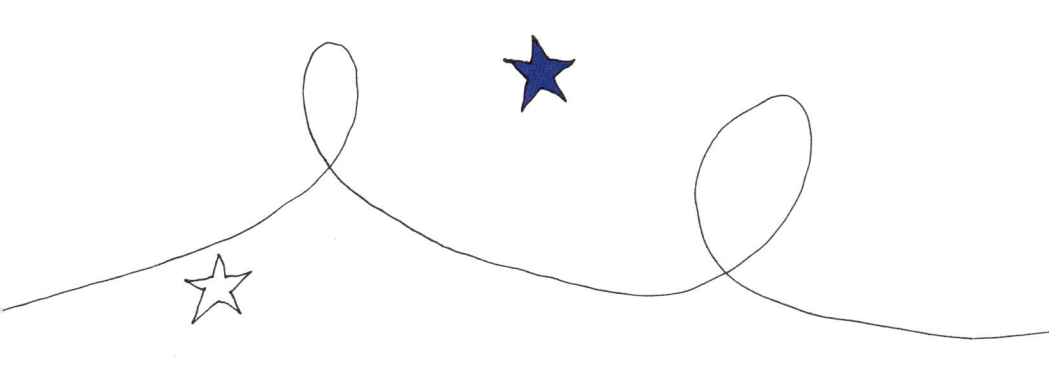

by Peter & Connie Roop / pictures by Joan Hanson

HOLLYWOOD

JAN 27 1994

ABL-7941
B-23 (112)
$11.95

DISCARDED BY
MEMPHIS PUBLIC LIBRARY

Lerner Publications Company · Minneapolis

To Sterling, our son, who has expanded our universe

Copyright © 1984 by Lerner Publications Company

All rights reserved. International copyright secured.
No part of this book may be reproduced in any form whatsoever
without permission in writing from the publisher except for
the inclusion of brief quotations in an acknowledged review.

Library of Congress Cataloging in Publication Data

Roop, Peter.
  Space out!

  (Make me laugh!)
  Summary: A collection of riddles and jokes about
outer space, including "What goes up when you count
down?" (a rocket) and "What do Martians have that no
one else can have?" (baby Martians).
  1. Outer space—anecdotes, facetiae, satire, etc.
2. Wit and humor, Juvenile. [1. Outer space—Wit and
humor. 2. Space flight—Wit and humor. 3. Extrater-
restrial beings—Wit and humor. 4. Riddles] I. Roop,
Connie, II. Hanson, Joan, ill. III. Title. IV. Series.
PN6231.S645R66   1984   818'.5402   84-5650
ISBN 0-8225-0984-9 (lib. bdg.)

Manufactured in the United States of America

    4 5 6 7 8 9 10 93 92 91 90 89

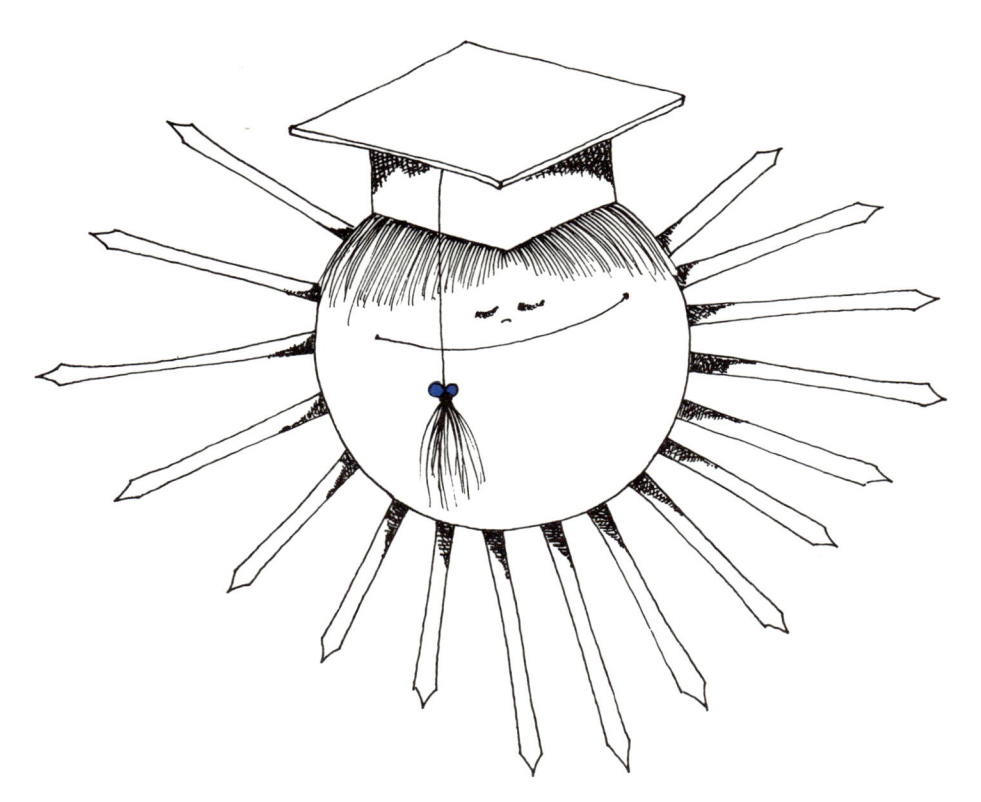

Q: Why is the sun the smartest star?
A: Because it's so bright.

Q: What do space squirrels like to eat?
A: Astro-nuts.

Q: What state has the most astronauts?
A: Moon-tana.

Mary: I'm going to be the first person to land on the sun.
Jerry: You can't do that, you'll burn up!
Mary: No I won't. I'll land at night!

Q: What's a space creature's favorite food?
A: Human beans.

Q: What does an astronaut shave with?
A: A laser razor.

Q: Why did the moon go to the bank?
A: To change quarters.

Q: What's the best way to talk to a martian?
A: By long distance!

Q: What kind of music do astronauts like?
A: Nep-tunes.

Q: Why did the sheriff put the star in jail?
A: It was a shooting star.

Q: If an athlete gets athlete's foot, what does an astronaut get?
A: Missile toe.

Q: How do you capture a fly from outer space?
A: Use a Venus flytrap.

Q: What kind of flowers can you find in space?
A: Sun-flowers.

Q: What do martians have that no one else can have?
A: Baby martians!

Q: What are the best days for astronauts to go into space?
A: Moon-day and Saturn-day.

Q: Why did the cow jump over the moon?
A: To get to the Milky Way.

Q: Why did the astronaut take a mop into space?
A: To clean up the stardust.

Boy: I saw something last night I couldn't get over.
Girl: What was that?
Boy: The moon.

First Scientist: I know a planet you can see both day and night.
Second Scientist: Really? Which one?
First Scientist: Earth.

Q: What goes up when you count down?
A: A rocket.

Q: What holds up the moon?
A: Moon beams.

Mother: Why are you going outside with an empty ice cream cone?
Son: I'm going to use the Big Dipper.

Q: What kind of years weigh the least?
A: Light years.

Q: Where do martians go fishing?
A: In the galax-seas.

Q: Why is the letter T so powerful?
A: It can make a star start.

Q: Why is the North Star the best star?
A: It outshines all the rest.

Q: What happens when a martian falls into a puddle?
A: He gets wet!

Q: Why do thin cowboys make good astronauts?
A: They're good at sitting in the saddle-light.

Q: Which is heavier, a full moon or a half moon?
A: A half moon. A full moon is lighter.

Q: How do astronauts get ready for a trip into space?
A: They have to "plan-it."

Q: Why should stars wear braces?
A: Because there's so much space between them.

Q: How does an astronaut keep up his pants?
A: With an asteroid belt!

Q: Why didn't the satellite go very far?
A: It kept going around in circles.

Q: Why did the astronaut take an American flag into space?
A: It was a star-spangled banner.

Q: How does the Man in the Moon cut his hair?
A: Eclipse-it.

Q: How is a telephone like the planet Saturn?
A: They both have rings.

Q: What's the difference between fog and a falling star?
A: One is mist on earth, and the other is missed in space.

Q: Why did the singer go up into space?
A: She wanted to become a star.

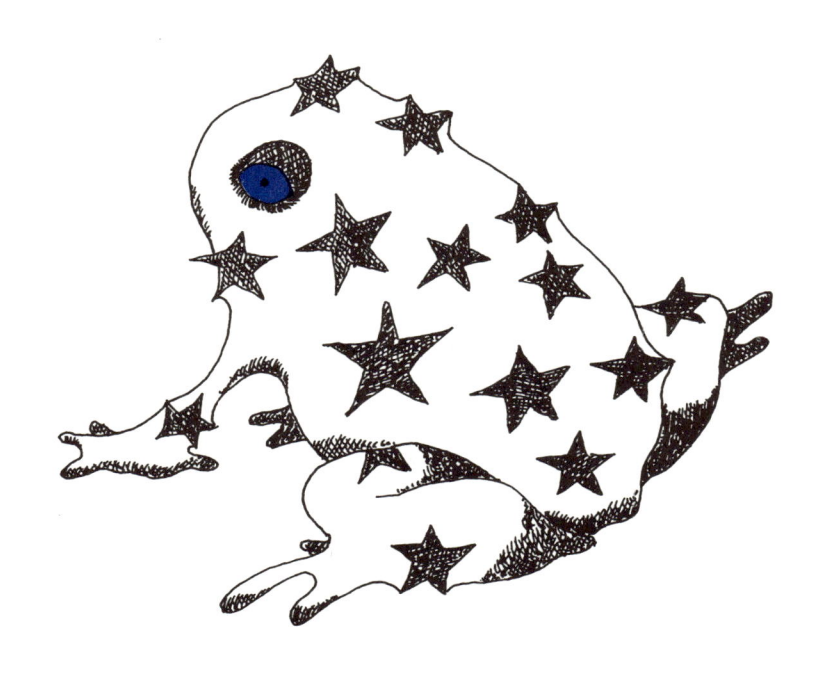

Q: What do space toads have all over their bodies?
A: Star warts!

Q: Why did the astronaut take a shovel into space?
A: To dig a black hole.

Q: What's an astronaut's favorite fish?
A: Starfish.

Q: Where do astronauts go to college?
A: U.F.O.—University for Orbiting.

Q: What time is it when a martian peeks in your window?
A: Time to close the blinds!

Q: What kind of shots do astronauts get?
A: Boosters.

Q: Why do astronauts enjoy space travel?
A: It's out of this world!

Q: What did the North Star say to the Big Dipper?
A: "It's not polite to point!"

Q: How do you know when the moon isn't hungry?
A: When it's full!

Q: What does the runner-up in the Ms. Galaxy contest receive?
A: A constellation prize.

Q: Which astronaut goes into space the most?
A: Sir Launch-alot.

Q: How did the sailor know there wasn't a Man in the Moon?
A: He'd already been to sea.

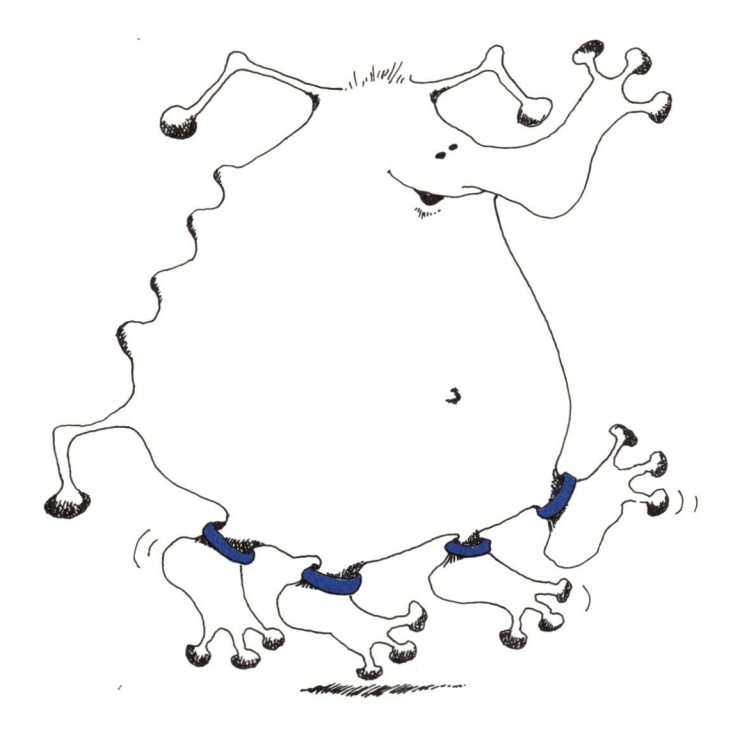

Q: Why can't a martian's nose be 12 inches long?
A: If it were, it would be a foot!

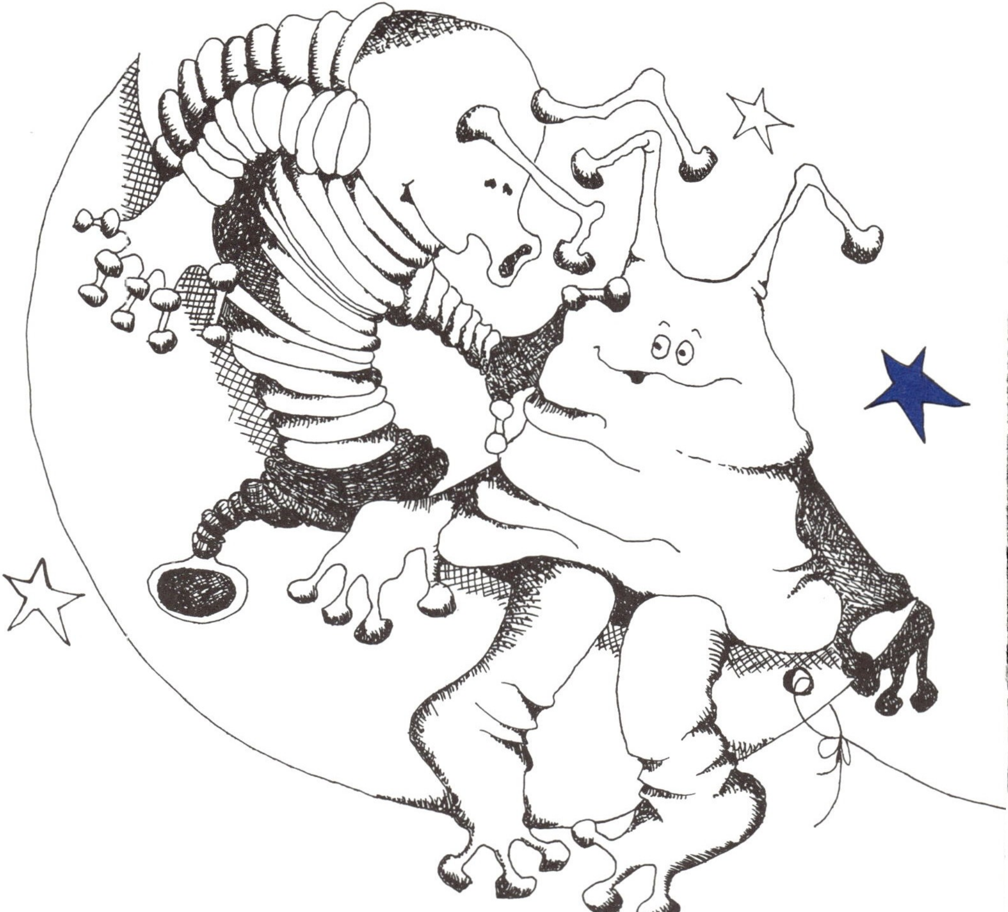

ABOUT THE AUTHORS

PETER AND CONNIE ROOP have enjoyed sharing jokes with students in the United States and Great Britain. When not joking around, Peter and Connie write books and articles. Traveling, camping, and reading with their children, Sterling and Heidi, are their favorite pastimes. Both graduates of Lawrence University, the Roops now live in Appleton, Wisconsin.

ABOUT THE ARTIST

JOAN HANSON lives with her husband and two sons in Afton, Minnesota. Her distinctive, deliberately whimsical pen-and-ink drawings have illustrated more than 30 children's books. Ms. Hanson is also an accomplished weaver. A graduate of Carleton College, Hanson enjoys tennis, skiing, sailing, reading, traveling, and walking in the woods surrounding her home.

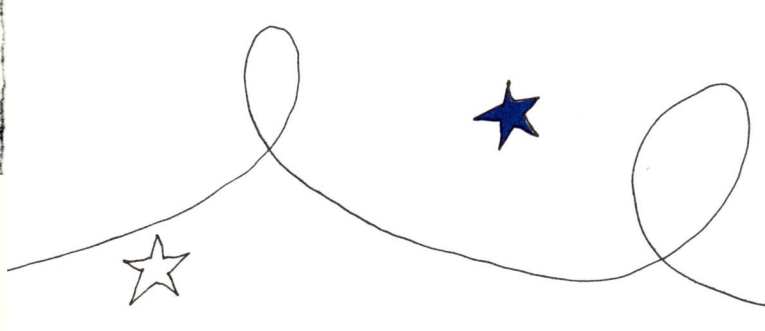

Make Me Laugh!

CAN YOU MATCH THIS?
CAT'S OUT OF THE BAG!
CLOWNING AROUND!
DUMB CLUCKS!
ELEPHANTS NEVER FORGET!
FACE THE MUSIC!
FOSSIL FOLLIES!
GO HOG WILD!
GOING BUGGY!
GRIN AND BEAR IT!
HAIL TO THE CHIEF!
IN THE DOGHOUSE!
KISS A FROG!
LET'S CELEBRATE!
OUT TO LUNCH!
OUT TO PASTURE!
SNAKES ALIVE!
SOMETHING'S FISHY!
SPACE OUT!
STICK OUT YOUR TONGUE!
WHAT A HAM!
WHAT'S YOUR NAME?
WHAT'S YOUR NAME, AGAIN?
101 ANIMAL JOKES
101 FAMILY JOKES
101 KNOCK-KNOCK JOKES
101 MONSTER JOKES
101 SCHOOL JOKES
101 SPORTS JOKES